Ribbons for
special occasions

Wrapping with elegance

Kumiko Nagai

NIHON VOGUE-SHA

C O N T E N T S

(COVER) Ribbon・Crossed Loop Bow(Pages 14-15) Iridescent organdy ribbon No.4563 75$^m/_m$ Col.7 Iridescent taffeta ribbon No.4595 25$^m/_m$ Col.11
(P.1, P.72) Ribbon・Crossed Loop Bow(Page 14) Iridescent organdy ribbon No.4563 100$^m/_m$ Col.1、12

All ribbons and most of the wrapping papers in the book are the products of **MOKUBA**.

(Remarks)
''In every picture, each product identified under the photo as follows:
● Ribbon: Tying Method (instruction page), Ribbon Name, Item No., Ribbon width, Color No.
● Wrapping paper: Wrapping Method (instruction page), Item No., Color No. (Only describes ''Wrapping'', in the case of non-MOKUBA products.)''

STAFF
Artdirector／KIYOSHI INANO＋TAZUKO MATSUMOTO (B.C.)
Photographer／HITOSHI OKUTANI
Editor／YUKO MURAKAMI
Associate Staff／MOMOKO YAMAGUCHI

Ribbons and bouquet

A festive bow

For that day of unbounded happiness, send your very best with flowers.

A bow in festive ribbon keeps the happiness from slipping away...

Ribbon・Classic Bow (Page 12) Frilled satin ribbon No.4895 50$_\text{m/m}$ Col.7

A chic bow in a color to match the petals

Ribbon · Single-loop Bow (Page 13) Velvet ribbon No.2500 15ᵐ/ₘ Col.53

(Picture : Above) Ribbon・Double Bow (Page 13) Taffeta ribbon with satin edges No.4495 25㎜ Col.64
(Picture : Below) Ribbon・Pretty-side-up Bow (Page 16) Floral jacquard ribbon No.4557 Col.15

A table aflutter with bows

She loves those dishes with the bow motif. She's sure to serve tonight's dinner on them.

Make sure your bouquet arrives a little early.

Ribbon • Crossed Loop Bow (Pages 14,15) Iridescent organdy ribbon No.4563 50ᵐ/m Col.7 Iridescent taffeta ribbon No.4595 25ᵐ/m Col.9

Ribbon・Classic Bow (Page 12) Pleated satin ribbon No.0492 6㎜ Col.16

A festive day sealed with a bow

Seal this day with a bow to send thanks words alone cannot express.

A wish for joy that never wearies.

S t y l e 1

Classic Bow

(Pages 4–5)

The most familiar way to tie a ribbon—and the most perfect. This basic technique produces a host of effects depending on the type of ribbon and its width.

1. Pass one end under the other and pull snug.

2. Pressing on the center of the knot, fold the right end forward and to the left, to form a loop.

3. Fold the left end down and across the loop; hold between the thumb and forefinger of your right hand.

4. Fold the left end in two and pass the fold beneath the first loop to form a second loop.

5. Hold the knot with a thumb while pulling on the loops to make a symmetrical, well-balanced bow.

6. Cut off ends to suit the size of the loops.

Style 2

Double Bow

(Page 7)

With two loops on each side, the bow becomes even more festive. The trick is to tie the first bow tightly.

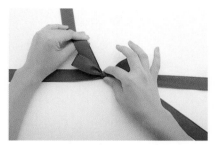

1. Create a Classic Bow by following steps 1-5 of the Classic Bow. Then, pressing on the knot with your right hand, lift the left end above the left loop.

2. Tie a second Classic Bow. Hold all four loops close to their bases and tug tightly.

3. Arrange the loops so that none overlap. Trim the ends.

Style 3

Single-loop Bow

(Page 6)

For a gift to a gentle man, or when you don't want the exterior of the gift to be too fancy, try this elegantly casual bow to add some spice to your wrapping.

1. Pass one end under the other and pull snug. Pressing on the center of the knot, fold the right end forward and to the left, to form a loop.

2. Fold the left end down and across the loop, then pass it beneath the first loop. Tug on that end and the loop to tighten the knot.

3. Arrange the loop and ends. Trim the ends so that they are in balance with the size of the loop.

13

Style 4

Crossed Loop Bow

(Pages 8-9)

This technique was created to make the most of lustrous iridescent ribbon. The trick is to have plenty of fullness in the loops before you twist them.

1. Fold back the ribbon to the rear as shown.

2. Bring the ribbon in your right hand to cross in the front, as shown, and hold with your left hand.

3. Carry that end down and back to form a V-shape, then fold back and cross again at the front.

4. Repeat steps 1 through 3 so that you have four loops of about the same size.

5. Pass a wire around the cross points so that its ends are on the right side. As you tighten the wire, draw up gathers in the ribbon. Wrap the wire around two or three times.

6. Cut the wire to leave 2 to 3 millimeter ends.

Style 5

Tying on a Crossed Loop Bow

(Pages 8-9)

1. *For the ties, use another length of the ribbon used for the Crossed Loop Bow. Knot once. Hold the center of the knot.*

2. *Place the center of the Crossed Loop Bow on the center of the knot and hold in place. (If you like, add loops of another ribbon, as shown on page 8, for a yet more cheerful effect.)*

3. *Tie the bow on with the ties, covering the wire.*

4. *Hold the bow up and bring the ties forward.*

5. *Knot firmly at the base so that the bow is lifted up.*

6. *Trim the ties so that their length suits the loops, and arrange the bow and ties so that they are attractively balanced.*

S t y l e 6

Pretty-side-up Bow
(Page 7)

This technique ensures that the right side will show when you tie a bow with a ribbon that has distinct right and wrong sides. If you spread the ends horizontally, the result will resemble a bow tie.

1. Pass one end under the other and pull snug. Twist so that the left end is upside-down and the right end is right-side up.

2. Pressing on the center of the knot, fold the right end forward and to the left, to form a loop. Make a second loop, about twice as large, with the left end. Hold both at their centers.

3. Lap the left loop over the right, as shown.

4. Bring the left loop forward and under the right loop to tie the bow.

5. Tug on the loops to tighten the knot. The underside of the ribbon will be showing on the left end. Twist to reverse it.

6. Trim the ends to suit the size of the loops. For a tailored effect, try spreading the ends out horizontally. Doesn't that look like a bow tie?

Ribbon Collection 1

Double-sided satin ribbon	Grosgrain ribbon (polyester)	Velvet ribbon
Picoted satin ribbon	Grosgrain ribbon (rayon)	Bright velvet ribbon
Organdy frilled satin ribbon	Iridescent grosgrain ribbon	Bright velvet ribbon
Pleated satin ribbon	Iridescent grosgrain ribbon	Pleated velvet ribbon
Frilled satin ribbon	Iridescent velvet ribbon	Velvet ribbon with metallic edges

Ribbons and goodies

July : Berries and bows

July's jewels, gift of the garden: lusciously tart berries. The plump fruit is a symbol of happiness.

Before the birds steal them, pick them, tie up the berry basket with a bow, and share them with friends.

Ribbon · Double Bow (Page 13) Lace ribbon No.3234 Col.12

Ribbon・Winged Bow (Page 24) Lace ribbon No.3234 Col.12、No.3237 Col.12

A dressy bow for a tea party

Ribbon・Sheaf Bow (Page 25) Wire edged ribbon No.10200 15㎜ Col.4

Invited to sip tea and catch up on your conversation? Bring a white cake to match your dress and add an extra touch with one of our collection of bows in canary, wild-rose.

Ribbon・Wave Loop Bow (Page 24) Frilled satin ribbon No.4895 21㎜ Col.40

Red ribbon wraps up a delicious gift.

These red-ribbon gifts are some of my favorite foods. White asparagus, olives... often playing a supporting role at the dinner table, they're in the limelight here.

All credits for the ribbons and wrapping papers on these pages appear on page 86.

S t y l e 7

Winged Bow
(Page 19)

This crisp, simple bow is perfect for an unassuming gift. The effect of its unadorned elegance can be formal, too. Try it with a rich velvet ribbon.

1. Pass one end under the other and pull snug. Fold the left end so that its tip faces right.

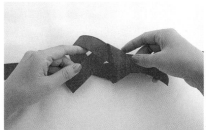

2. While holding the left end at the bend, lift the right end above the left and pull it through the left end's bend, to form a square knot.

3. Pull the left and right ends snug to tighten the knot, then pull them above it and trim.

S t y l e 8

Wave Loop Bow
(Page 21)

This simple technique needs only a staple at one point to create a perky bow. It's ideal where tying with a ribbon would be difficult: an accent on a pretty carrier bag, for instance.

1. Form a thumb-sized loop at one end, coiling the end clockwise. With the trailing end of the ribbon, form two more loops, top and bottom, behind the first one.

2. Adjust the loops so that they are centered and their edges are in a straight line. Secure with a staple at the back of the center loop, as shown.

3. Cut off the ends so that they don't show. Place on the gift with double-stick tape.

Style 9

Sheaf Bow

(Page 20)

This simple technique creates a delight-ful multi-looped bow without wire. It can add a festive touch to any gift.

1. Pass one end under the other and pull snug, with the right end much longer. Pressing on the knot, fold the right end to form a loop. Hold it in place with a finger at the knot.

2. With the right end, form another loop on the other side of the knot. Hold in place with a finger at the knot.

3. Repeat to form more loops with the right end. You should have the same number of loops on both sides of the knot.

4. Bring the left end to the front, wrap across all the loops at the knot and around in back. Knot the left and right ends.

5. Pressing on the center, pull the knot snug.

6. Plump out each loop and your sheaf bow is finished. For extra bounce, try curling the ends before you trim them.

S t y l e 10

"Bagging" It
(Pages 22-23)

Bagging them is a deft solution to wrapping cans, bottles, and other awkward shapes. If you prefer, make your bag deeper, to hide the contents.

1. Prepare the paper as shown on page 77. Place the gift to be wrapped in the center.

2. Fold the left and front sides straight up.

3. Bring together at the corner and fold so the flap is at the front.

4. Repeat for the right side. Tape down the left and right flaps.

5. Staple where the flaps overlap. Repeat steps 1-5 for the other side.

6. Circle the completed bag with ribbon and tie into a bow.

Ribbon Collection 2

Picoted organdy ribbon	Pleated iridescent organdy ribbon	Iridescent rayon ribbon
Speciality weave organdy ribbon	Organdy ribbon	Taffeta with herringbone trim ribbon
Iridescent organdy ribbon	Metallic-printed organdy ribbon	Taffeta with decorative dots ribbon
Satin-edged organdy ribbon	Rayon ribbon	Iridescent taffeta ribbon
Metallic-printed organdy ribbon	Picoted taffeta ribbon	Cotton ribbon

Ribbons for formal occasions

A perfect bow

For a formal gift—to a teacher, perhaps—nothing suits as well as a bow in luxurious velvet on pure white paper.

The restraint and care that lie behind the simplicity of the presentation will communicate your sincerity.

Ribbon • Pretty-side-up Bow (Page 16) Iridescent velvet ribbon No.4583 40m/m Col.8
Wrapping paper • Diagonal Wrapping for a Deep Box (Page 36) WP003 Col.2

Ribbon・Pretty-side-up Bow (Page 16) Iridescent velvet ribbon No.4583 25㎜ Col.8

A bow that says "thank-you"

A longed-for letter from an absent parent —how better to express your thanks than to send a custom letter set (to encourage more letters!), wrapped in grateful love.

Let that loving grandmother know just how much her gift was appreciated. A snapshot of the happy grandchild with it, framed, wrapped, and sealed with a bow, says it all.

(Picture : Above) Ribbon • Crossed Loop Bow (Pages 14,15)＋Curling (Page 85) Metallic organdy ribbon No.4569 25ᵐ/m、38ᵐ/m Col.1
(Picture : Below) Ribbon • Crossed Loop Bow (Pages 14,15) Iridescent rayon ribbon No.4599 35ᵐ/m Col.10,11
Wrapping • Diagonal Wrapping for a Shallow Box (Page 37)

(Box : Left) Ribbon・Sheaf Bow (Page 25) Braid with metallic threads No.4594 Col.95　Wrapping・Square Wrapping (Page 75)

(Box : Right) Ribbon・Single-loop Bow (Page 13) Herringbone ribbon No.4593 Col.95

Wrapping・Classic Box Wrapping with Pleats (Page 77)

That signature bow

(Wrapping : Left) Ribbon • Crossed Loop Bow (Pages 14,15)
Iridescent metallic organdy ribbon No.4617 38㎜ Col.5 Iridescent taffeta ribbon No.4595 38㎜ Col.16
Wrapping paper • Pleating a Cylinder (Page 38) WP007 Col.56

Gifts throughout the seasons, each carring your signature ribbon and bow, bring the message that you are unchanging in your affections. To a distant friend, they're the next best thing to seeing your smiling face.

(Wrapping : Right) Ribbon • Classic Bow (Page 12) Picoted taffeta ribbon No.4522 52m/m Col.7
Wrapping paper • Diagonally Wrapping a Cylinder (Page 39) WP007 Col.8

White garlands of happiness

On that day when all the happiness in the world was hers, she wept—and laughed—with joy.
And even greater joy awaits her.

All credits for the ribbons and wrapping papers on these pages appear on page 86.

Style 11

Diagonal Wrapping for a Deep Box

(Page 28)

For a relatively deep box, wrap it using a technique that lets you hold the box relatively still in the process. This basic technique has a wide range of applications; take the time to master it now.

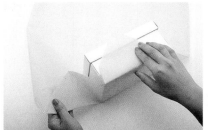

1. Prepare the paper as shown on page 75. Lift the front flap up to cover. Bring the left-hand side straight up, folding excess paper to the inside, and cover the top.

2. Tape it down. Bring up the rear flap, folding excess paper to the inside, and turn the box on its end, aligning the folded edge with the edge of the box, as shown.

3. While holding as shown, turn the box and paper to stand on the rear side.

4. Bring up the paper on the right-hand straight up, folding excess paper to the inside, and bring up to cover the top.

5. While holding the right-side paper in place, adjust the paper in the rear so that its folded edges do not extend beyond the edges of the box, and bring it up over the top.

6. Secure with double-stick tape.

Style 12

Diagonal Wrapping for a Shallow Box

(Page 30)

This wrapping technique has many uses. Its formal effect makes it suitable for the most ceremonial of occasions. Since it also works with almost any type of bow, the possibilities are endless.

1. Prepare paper (see p.74). Fold front flap up to cover box top. Fold L-side straight up, folding in excess paper. Cover top, aligning crease with box edge.

2. Secure with tape. Turn the box on its back as shown while folding the paper at the back to the inside.

3. Adjust so that the folded edge aligns with the edge of the box, then turn the box once more.

4. Turn the box right-side up. Fold the paper along the right side straight up, folding excess paper to the inside and aligning the folded edge with the edge of the box. Bring up to cover the top.

5. Bring up the rear flap to cover the upper surface in the same way, folding excess paper to the inside.

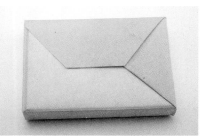

6. Overlap the rear flap with the front flap, fold the edges in, and secure with double-stick tape. (Leaving the edges unfolded is also fine.)

Style 13

Pleating a Cylinder
(Page 32)

This technique is effective for wrapping a round box with a relatively large diameter. It takes skill, but the effect of the pleats neatly gathered at the center is elegant indeed.

1. Prepare paper (see p.78). Put double stick tape 2mm from R-edge at center. Prepare 2 seals with the same paper & double stick tape.

2. Place side of box on paper's center (see 1). Bring up L, then R-sides and secure with double stick tape. Gently fold bottom paper under.

3. Starting with the inner layer of paper, form pleats, aiming at the center.

4. Fold the last pleat inside at an angle.

5. Hold in place with the seal prepared in step 1.

6. Turn upside down, lift up the temporarily folded paper, and pleat, making the pleats run the opposite direction. Hold in place with the other seal.

Style 14

Diagonally Wrapping a Cylinder

(Page 32)

This technique is recommended for a cylinder you can easily hold in your hand. The pleats produce a charming rounded shape.

1. *Prepare the paper as shown on page 78. Set the cylinder diagonally on the paper, near one corner, turn the corner up to cover it, and hold with your right hand.*

2. *Gather up small pleats that angle towards your right index finger. Continue about half way around.*

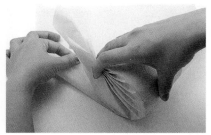

3. *Fold excess paper on the left to the inside and roll the cylinder slightly. Next fold to the inside the paper that is sticking out at the front and roll the cylinder more.*

4. *Repeat step 2 for the right side.*

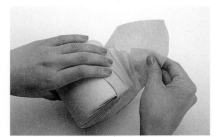

5. *Keep any remaining paper from extending above the edges of the cylinder by folding to the inside as you roll the cylinder.*

6. *To hold the handsome pleats in place, tape the end with double-stick tape.*

S t y l e 15

Pleating a Plate

(Pages 34-35)

This technique wraps a round plate in square paper. Casual pleats are more chic than rigidly accurate ones.

1. Prepare the paper as shown on page 78. Place the plate in the center. Bring up the front corners and begin making pleats pointed at the center, working towards the left.

2. Continue pleating to the left. The paper extending beyond the plate's center point should be folded inside.

3. Now pleat to the right in the same way. At the top of the plate, lift up the paper in a triangle.

4. Again fold paper extending beyond the plate's center to the inside. Pleat the triangle of paper you lifted up in step 3.

5. Pull on and neaten the remaining corner. Fold the part of it extending beyond the plate's center to the inside.

6. Hold the end in place with double-stick tape.

Style 16

Pleating a Cup and Saucer

(Pages 34-35)

This wrapping technique is so charming that the wrapping could stand on its own as a gift. It's an excellent way to deal with irregular shapes, such as a cup and saucer.

1. Put a sheet of paper between the cup and saucer. Prepare the paper as shown on page 78. Place the cup and saucer in the center and fold up the front side to cover, as shown.

2. Pleat from the front to the right, gathering the paper at the center of the cup.

3. After pleating halfway around, hold the paper gathered at the center with your right hand.

4. Pleat the other half in the same way, starting from the front.

5. Hold all the gathered paper in your left hand and temporarily secure with wire.

6. Tie a bow and remove the wire.

Style 17

Figure Eight Bow
(Page 42)

This technique uses wire to hold loops in which the right side of the ribbon is always showing. The effect can be dazzling even with soft or sheer ribbon.

1. With ribbon ends in each hand, overlap to form a loop. Holding that loop with L-thumb, loop again forming a figure-8, (right sides showing).

2. Repeat to create two more loops. Secure with wire where your thumb has been holding the loops in place. Cut the ends of the wire to 2-3 millimeters.

3. See the instructions on page 15 (5. Attaching a Crossed Loop Bow) to attach the bow. Trim the ends.

Style 18

Ribbon Frill
(Pages 34-35)

This extra frill accents a bow made with a different ribbon. Keep a close eye on the size of your loops for a well-bred frill.

1. Complete a double bow (page 13) and lift up its loops and ends. Drape a separate ribbon around its base, as shown.

2. Pull the second ribbon strongly towards you, then tie a classic bow.

3. Adjust the size of its loops to suit the first bow and trim the ends to match.

Ribbon Collection 3

Tartan check ribbon	Striped organdy ribbon	Polka-dotted organdy ribbon (pin dots)
Check ribbon	Picoted striped ribbon	Rose jacquard ribbon
Taffeta ribbon with satin edges	Polka-dotted satin ribbon	Picoted floral jacquard ribbon
Gingham check ribbon	Polka-dotted organdy ribbon	Floral jacquard ribbon
Striped ribbon	Polka-dotted taffeta ribbon	Floral jacquard ribbon

Ribbons for someone special

Your favorite color of ribbon

Ribbon・Single-loop Bow (Page 13) Velvet ribbon No.2500 25㎜ Col.44

For that special present, a special ribbon.

Tie it with ribbon in your favorite color instead of enclosing a card.

The message is clear: your hearts are bound together.

Ribbon · Classic Bow Variation (Page 50) Velvet ribbon No.2500 38㎜ Col.44

The ribbon orchestrates a symphony of gift-giving

Ribbon • Pretty-side-up Bow (Page 16) Floral jacquard ribbon No.4847 Col.5   Wrapping • Classic Box Wrapping (Page 76)

On that special evening, these clever ribbons orchestrate a symphony of romantic gift-giving. Here the ribbons
are in charge—but they need your help to pull off the effect.

(Picture : Left) Ribbon • Single-loop Bow (Page 13) Double-sided satin ribbon No.1100 24㎜ Col.32
Wrapping • Classic Box Wrapping with Pleats (Page 77)
(Picture : Right) Ribbon • Single-loop Bow (Page 13) Braid with metallic threads No.5287 Col.3
Wrapping • Classic Box Wrapping with Pleats (Page 77)

Pink ribbons for her

Ribbon • Wired Loop Bow (Page 52) Striped ribbon No.4832 Col.5、No.4833 Col.5

Wrapping paper • Pleating a Cylinder (Page 38) WP003 Col.2

"A Marie Melchier hat would be
perfect with that pink dress I bought
at Saint Nolet, don't you think?"
With her birthday near,
she's hinting as usual.

Her university graduation is several
years in the past, but she is eternally
the fresh young thing. Her friends
hope she'll never lose her bow-like
perky grace.

(Picture : Above) Ribbon • Twisted Loop Bow (Page 51) Polka-dotted organdy ribbon No.4865 Col.40

(Picture : Below) Ribbon • Classic Bow (Page 12) Single-face satin ribbon No.1150 3㎜ Col.40

Style 19

Classic Bow Variation
(Page 45)

Tying this bow takes skill, but it keeps the right side out for ribbons with two distinct sides. It also produces a strikingly straight center section.

1. Tie ends: L-end down & R-end up. With the R, form a large loop with the end angled. Secure at center.

2. Fold the left end down and across the loop; hold between the thumb and forefinger of your right hand.

3. Pass the same end around the loop down and across again to the left.

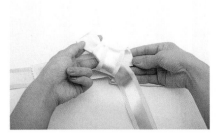

4. There are now two loops circling the first one. Lift up the right-hand loop and pass it over the left.

5. Tug on the two loops to tighten the knot and make a symmetrical, well-balanced bow.

6. Trim the ends.

S t y l e 20

Twisted Loop Bow

(Page 49)

These large loops are strikingly bold. Try them when you want an uninhibitedly outgoing effect.

1. Form a thumb-sized loop at one end, coiling the end clockwise. Hold in the left hand. With the trailing end of the ribbon in your right hand, twist as shown before holding at the center.

2. Form another loop with the right end, at the rear. Twist before bringing the ribbon to the center to hold the loop.

3. Repeat, forming another loop above the first loop. Twist before bringing the ribbon to the center to the hold the loop.

4. Repeat steps 2 and 3, increasing the size of the loops, to make two more on each side of the first loop.

5. Decide length of trailing ends. Make a loop 2X the length of intended trail. Overlap loop at the back. Insert a wire where loops are held & twist.

6. Cut excess wire. Cut the last long loop in half to form trail ends. Pass another ribbon between the loops & the trailing ends. Then tie to the gift.

S t y l e 21

Wired Loop Bow

(Page 48)

This technique creates a circular bow with the loops radiating from a central point and the ribbon right-side up in all loops. Roundedness is the key concept here.

1. With the trailing end of the ribbon, form a loop to the rear and cross the short end as shown. Hold at the cross point.

2. Fold the trailing end to the front to form another loop, its base at the cross point.

3. Move the trailing end to the rear and fold to form another loop, its base at the cross point.

4. Form another loop at the front. Keep all the loops the same size.

5. Wrap the center with wire, twist, and cut off the wire's ends to about 2-3 millimeters.

6. Attach as for the Crossed Loop Bow (page 15). Trim the ties so that their length suits the loops, and arrange the bow and ties so that they are attractively balanced.

Ribbon Collection 4

Metallic organdy ribbon with dotted edges	Iridescent moire grosgrain ribbon	Wired taffeta ribbon
Metallic organdy ribbon	Moire grosgrain ribbon	Wired taffeta ribbon
Organdy ribbon with metallic edges	Moire ribbon	Wired taffeta ribbon with metallic edges
Iridescent metallic organdy ribbon	Two-toned moire ribbon	Lace ribbon
Braid with metallic threads	Iridescent moire ribbon with dotted edges	Metallic lace ribbon

Ribbons for little angels

Plaid ribbons for Christmas

Christmas brings out the champion shoppers in all of us. The festive atmosphere of the stores, the alluring displays, the joy of giving—it's so tempting to give one's self up to the pleasures of shopping.

All credits for the ribbons and wrapping papers on these pages appear on page 86.

Seal the package with a bow full of mother's love.

Ribbon · Double Bow (Page 13)＋Perky Petit Bow (Page 60) Polka-dotted satin ribbon No.4700 16㎜ Col.7
Wrapping paper · Classic Box Wrapping with Pleats (Page 77) WP006 Col.23

When that little girl has grown up, how many of the presents her parents gave her will she remember?

Tying the ribbons on each gift is the happiest moment.
Each bow carries a heartfelt wish :
"Oh, don't let my baby grow up too fast."

(Picture : Left) Ribbon • Double Bow (Page 13)＋Perky Pettit Bow (Page 60) Picoted satin ribbon No.1600 9㎜ Col.23
Wrapping • Classic Box Wrapping (Page 76)

(Picture : Right) Ribbon • Classic Bow (Page 12)＋Wired Bow (Page 60) Tubular grosgrain ribbon No.4500 15㎜ Col.46,50

The future with bows on

When the stork delivers a new life, why not celebrate the special day with a baby ring set with a petit birth stone?

It will please the proud mother—and be a lasting memento of an unforgettable day.

Ribbon • Classic Bow (Page 12) Grosgrain ribbon No.8900 6m/m Col.23

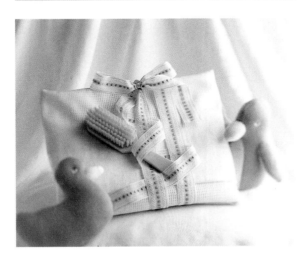

(Picture : Above) Ribbon • Classic Bow (Page 12) Organdy frilled satin ribbon No.4512 18㎜ Col.23

Wrapping paper • "Bagging" It (Page 26) WP003 Col.2

(Picture : Center) Ribbon • Wired Rose (Page 61) Wired Taffeta ribbon No.10100 25㎜ Col.2,15㎜ Col.2,32,34 Wire edged ribbon No.10200 15㎜ Col.11

(Picture : Below) Ribbon • Classic Bow (Page 12) Jacquard ribbon No.4891 Col.2   Wrapping • Classic Box Wrapping (Page 76)

Style 22

Perky Petit Bow

(Page 56)

Try this technique when you want to make a statement with narrow ribbon. It's charming for a child's gift or, perhaps, a gift of cookies.

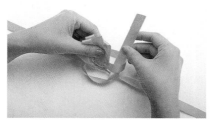

1. Make a Double Bow (page 13), leaving the right end rather long. Lift up the bow, circle its base with the long end, and pass the end through the loop thus formed.

2. Pull tightly on that end to draw in the base of the bow and make the bow stand up.

3. Adjust the ends to suit the size of the loops.

Style 23

Wired Bow

(Page 57)

To use this technique, insert a wire in hollow-woven grosgrain ribbon. It lets you shape the ribbon to your heart's delight.

1. Pass one end under the other and pull snug. The ends should be rather long. Insert a wire in each.

2. Tie a classic bow with the wired ribbon, then shape the ends. Use a pencil to curl them or fold them for a zigzag effect.

3. Arrange the ends amusingly.

60

S t y l e 24

Wired Rose

(Page 59)

The delicacy of wired ribbon, with its subtle colors, creates lovely artificial roses. A single bud or a bouquet—either is lovely.

1. Pull on the wire in the right-hand end to gather the ribbon. (Use 25 mm wide ribbon; about 20 centimeters is needed per rose.)

2. Make a triangular fold in the right-hand end. (You will cut off the excess wire at the end.)

3. Wrap from that end towards the inside to create the tightly furled heart of the flower.

4. Continue to wind the ribbon around the heart while forming more gathers. Shape to resemble a rose.

5. Cut off the ribbon diagonally and wrap the base twice with wire. Take both lengths of excess wire from the ends and wrap around the base. Twist tightly.

6. Cut off the excess wire. Finish with a pair of leaves: fold a ribbon, attach wire at the fold, and cut with pinking shears to create serrated edges.

Sending your favorites with ribbons

Garlands for a late weekend night.

Ribbon • Pretty-side-up Bow (Page 16) Polka-dotted taffeta ribbon No.4702 50㎜ Col.7

Rather than telling the story, let him read the book.
Rather than explaining, let her listen to the music.
Rather than giving away the ending, let them see the movie.

For a weekend with a good friend, bring along that deeply moving film you'd like to share. But plan to be talking 'til dawn.

(Picture : Above) Ribbon · Classic Bow (Page 12) Iridescent taffeta ribbon No.4595 9㍉ Col.3
(Picture : Below) Ribbon · Classic Bow (Page 12) Iridescent rayon ribbon No.4599 36㍉ Col.2

Autumnal tones and natural-colored ribbons

For a housewarming, plan with your friends to come up with the perfect gift. She'll love small accessories for the home in natural colors and fragrances. Why not celebrate with fresh scents and undyed ribbons for her new home?

All credits for the ribbons and wrapping papers on these pages appear on page 87.

Ribbons for happy toasts

Pair a red wine with a dandified cheese, and finish with cotton ribbon: the perfect combination.

On the day you discover a cherry-decorated liqueur glass, who could resist buying a bottle of Kirsch, too?

(Picture : Left) Ribbon・Single-loop Bow(Page13) Cotton ribbon No.1502 5㎜ Col.11
(Picture : Right) Ribbon・ Satin cord No.0927 Col. 15

Set the bottle of champagne in the wine cooler—and don't forget its bow tie.
There's no doubt who'll be the best dressed tonight.

Ribbon・Classic Bow Variation (Page 50) Velvet ribbon with metallic edges No.4592 25㎜ Col.34

Frothy ribbons

All credits for the ribbons and wrapping papers on these pages appear on page 87.

S t y l e 25

Wrapping a Bottle
(Page 68)

This technique wraps up the whole bottle, then finishes it with a bow at the neck. Experiment with types of paper and ribbons—the effect can be formal or light and amusing.

1. Prepare paper as shown on page 79. Lift up the paper at the front to cover the bottle, roll slightly, and pinch the paper at the base.

2. Using your index finger as the focal point, make pleats along about half the base.

3. Turn the excess paper inside, so that it does not stick out beyond the base. Fold the long edge of the paper inside and secure with double-stick tape.

4. Stand the bottle up, fold down the paper at the top two or three times, and secure with double-stick tape.

5. The wrapped bottle.

6. Add a ribbon around the neck.

S t y l e 26

Petal Wrapping

(Page 68)

Sometimes a box needs softer, plumper wrapping. This technique gives even small presents fullness and a festive air.

1. Prepare paper (see p.76). Follow instructions for classic wrapping, leaving extra length on L-end. Place box so front flap will reach box center.

2. Overlap the front and back flaps and secure with double-stick tape. Make creases to extend the lines of all four corners.

3. Fold the right flap along the creases and bring up to the top, keeping its edges just along the edges of the box top.

4. Softly fold up the extra paper on the left end. Gather for fullness across the box top.

5. Temporarily secure with wire.

6. Tie with a bow, remove the wire, and spread and shape the gathered paper ends to suggest petals.

A Dictionary of Wrapping Techniques

WRAPPING & TYING

This section systematically presents the wrapping and tying techniques shown in the color pages. Use them to create your own wrappings for that special day.

◆ *Wrapping Techniques*

Diagonal Wrapping for a Shallow Box
Diagonal Wrapping for a Deep Box
Square Wrapping
Classic Box Wrapping
Classic Box Wrapping with a Pocket
Classic Box Wrapping with Pleats
"Bagging" It
Diagonally Wrapping a Cylinder
Pleating a Cylinder
Wrapping a Bottle Diagonally
Wrapping a Bottle
Pleating a Plate
Pleating a Cup and Saucer
Pleating a Bottle

◆ *Tying Techniques*

Classic Bow
Double Bow
Pretty-side-up Bow
Classic Bow Variation
Winged Bow
Single-loop Bow
Sheaf Bow
Crossed Loop Bow
Wired Loop Bow
Figure Eight Bow
Twisted Loop Bow
Tying on a looped bow
Perky Petit Bow
Ribbon Frill
Inserted Bow
Combined Bow
Curling
Wave Loop Bow
Wired Rose
Wired Bow
Crossed Tying
Diagonal Tying
Triangular Tying
Single Tying

Wrapping Techniques
Diagonal and Square Wrapping

◆**Diagonal Wrapping for a Shallow Box** One of the most basic wrapping techniques (Cf. Page 37)

●**Paper size**

It's correct if front flap covers L-hand corner on the box front (see L. diagram), & rear flap covers the lower R. & upper L. corners on the front (shown below). If not, paper is too small. If larger, make initial overlap deeper with excess tucked underneath at the end.

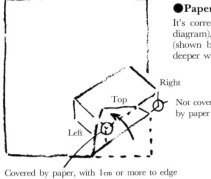

Right

Top

Not covered by paper

Left

Covered by paper, with 1cm or more to edge

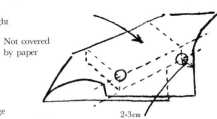

2-3cm

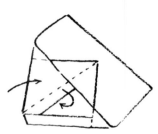

1. Fold the front flap up over the box top. Now fold up the paper along the left side and secure with tape.

2. Fold the paper inside as shown at(1) so that the circled corner barely shows. Turn the box on its back.

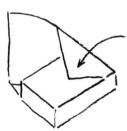

3. Adjusting the folded edge of the paper, turn the box once more.

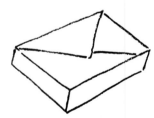

4. With the box right-side up, fold the paper along the right side up and over the top.

5. Fold the rear flap up and over the top. Secure with double-stick tape. (The rear corner may also be folded inside.)

◆**Square Wrapping** This technique is good for irregular objects, or those that should not be moved in wrapping.

●**Paper Size**

a＝box height＋2-3cm

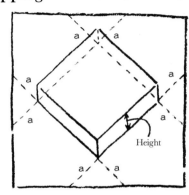

Height

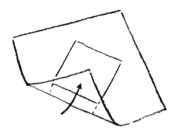

1. Place the object on the paper as shown and fold the front flap up over its top.

2. Fold paper's L-side over box top. Fold in any paper exceeding the extended diagonal of the box corners.

This technique enables you to wrap boxes with minimal disturbance to their contents by placing the box on the paper diagonally and folding the paper at each corner in turn. Once mastered, it is fast and fool proof.

◆**Diagonal Wrapping for a Deep Box** This technique uses the diagonal approach without rotating the box. (Cf. Page 36)

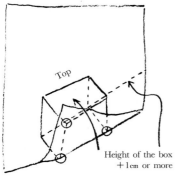
Top

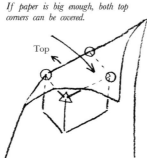
If paper is big enough, both top corners can be covered.
Top

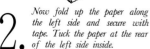
Height of the box +1cm or more

●**Paper size**
Turn box on back & put on paper as shown; i.e. front flap covers circled corners as per diagram (far left). Next check that rear flap covers same corners as per diagram (left). If not, paper is too small. If larger, make initial overlap deeper with excess tucked underneath at the end.

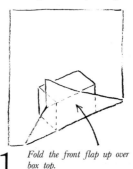
1. *Fold the front flap up over the box top.*

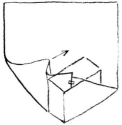
2. *Now fold up the paper along the left side and secure with tape. Tuck the paper at the rear of the left side inside.*

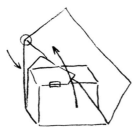
3. *Holding the box at the point indicated with the circle, turn the box and paper to stand on the rear side.*

4. *With the box right-side up, fold the paper along the right side up and over the top.*

5. *Fold the rear flap up and over the top. Secure with double-stick tape. (The rear corner may also be folded inside.)*

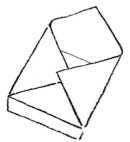
3. *Repeat step 2 for the paper on the right side.*

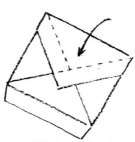
4. *Fold the rear flap up over the top. Fold underneath any paper extending beyond the two diagonals.*

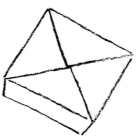
5. *Secure with double-stick tape.*

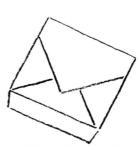
6. *Try this as a variation.*

Wrapping Techniques
— Classic Box Wrapping and Variations —

◆**Classic Box Wrapping** This basic technique makes it simple to see where the paper will be positioned, to bring out its pattern most effectively.

●**Paper size**

paper length depends on end flap usage.
Using Petal Wrapping variation (p.71) length = 2 × (Circumference + 10 cm).

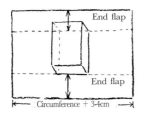

End flap treatments

A. For a deep, nearly square box

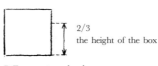

2/3 the height of the box

B. For a rectangular box

3/4 the height of the box

C. For a shallow rectangular box

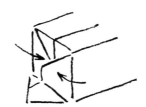

Height of the box + 1 cm

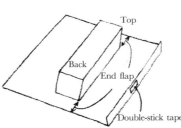

1. *Fold the right-hand edge in and place double-stick tape at its center.*

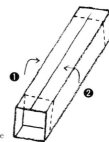

2. *Fold up the sides in the order shown and secure with the tape readied in step 1.*

A. For a deep, nearly square box

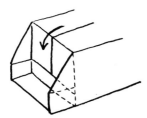

3. *Fold paper down at top edges. Make diagonal creases in the resulting side flaps.*

4. *At one end, fold the left and right side flaps in neatly. A triangle will be formed facing towards you. Crease its sides.*

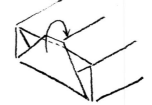

5. *Fold the triangle up and secure with double-stick tape. Repeat steps 4-5 for the other end.*

C. For a shallow rectangular box

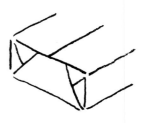

3. *Neatly fold the paper at each end along the edges of the box, working in this order: left, right, top, and bottom.*

B. For a rectangular box

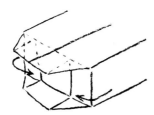

3. *Fold the paper along the vertical sides of the box ends. Crease the resulting upper & lower flaps along the box edges.*

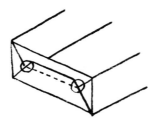

4. *Fold the upper and lower flaps as shown. Fold the edge where they overlap underneath (see the circles).*

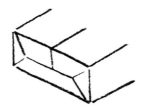

5. *Secure with double-stick tape.*

4. *Fold any paper that shows at the top of the box underneath and secure with double-stick tape.*

In classic box wrapping, the edges of the paper parallel the box edges. It's especially useful for heavy or awkward objects. The possible variations are endless—master the basics, and you'll be able to design your own.

◆Classic Box Wrapping with a Pocket An example of wrapping with a cross pocket.

● **Paper Size**

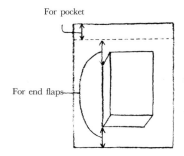

For pocket

For end flaps

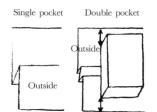

Single pocket   Double pocket

Outside

Outside

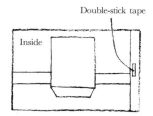

Inside

Double-stick tape

1. *Fold tucks into the paper—once for a single pocket, twice for a double one, and so on. Make sure you leave enough paper for the end flaps.*

2. *Proceed with Classic Box Wrapping (page 76), folding up both sides and securing with double-stick tape.*

3. *Fold in the end flaps and secure with double-stick tape.*

◆Classic Box Wrapping with Pleats An example of lengthwise pleated wrap.

● **Paper size**

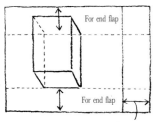

For end flap

For end flap

For pleats
Use between 5 cm and the width of the box top for the pleats.

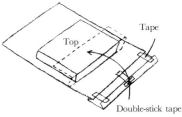

Top

Tape

Double-stick tape

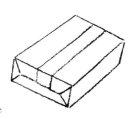

Accordion pleats

Diagonal pleats

Box pleats

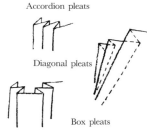

1. *Form pleats at the right edge, tape in place, and position double-stick tape at the center.*

2. *Proceed with Classic Box Wrapping (page 76).*

3. *Experiment with these pleat types.*

◆"Bagging" It Bagging them is a quick way to wrap irregularly shaped objects.(Cf. Page 26)

● **Paper Size**

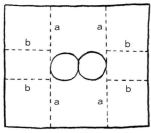

a   a
b   b
b   b
a   a

"a" should be equal to "b" or longer (about 1.5 times as long)

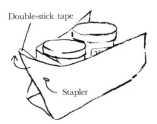

Double-stick tape

Stapler

1. *At one end, bring the left side straight up and fold as shown.*

2. *Repeat for the right side. Staple where the flaps overlap.*

3. *Repeat steps 1-2 for the other end.*

Wrapping Techniques
— Pleated Wrapping —

◆**Diagonally Wrapping a Cylinder** This Technique is the most orthodox way of wrapping a cylinder. (Cf.Page 39)

●**Paper Size**

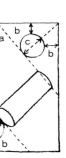

a = circumference
    + 4-5cm

b = 4-5cm

c = diameter

 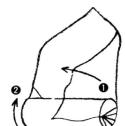 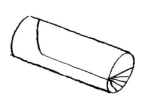

1. *Set cylinder on paper. Turn closest corner and cover. Gather small pleats with 1 focal point. Fold paper to inside rear in the order shown.*

2. *Fold in pleats at the other end of the cylinder. Fold the paper to the rear to the inside in the order shown.*

3. *Adjust folds to clean up the shape and secure with double-stick tape.*

◆**Pleating a Cylinder** This technique is good for a cylindrical object with a relatively large diameter.(Cf.Page 38)

●**Paper size**

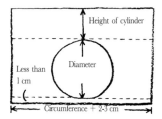

  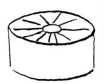

1. *Wrap the paper around the cylinder as shown and secure with double-stick tape. Gently fold under the paper for the bottom.*

2. *Starting with the inner layer of paper, form pleats, aiming at the center.*

3. *Fold the last pleat inside at an angle. Secure with a seal made of the same paper. Repeat for the bottom.*

◆**Pleating a Plate** This technique also creates pleats radiating out from the center.(Cf.Page 40)

●**Paper size**

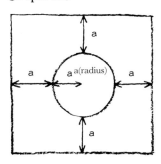

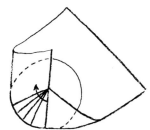 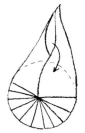 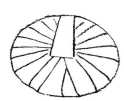

1. *Bring up the front corners and begin making pleats pointed at the center, working towards the left.*

2. *Repeat, working towards the right. Lift the corner at the back and make more pleats.*

3. *Fold down the triangle of paper that forms at the back. The flap that extends beyond center - fold under & secure.*

These techniques are solutions to wrapping bottles and other irregularly shaped objects. Pleating along the surface of the object to accent its shape creates a handsome wrapping effect. Master the technique and you'll be able to wrap almost anything with style.

◆Wrapping a Bottle Diagonally This technique is the orthodox way of wrapping a bottle.

●**Paper Size**

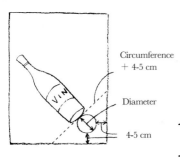

Circumference
+ 4-5 cm

Diameter

4-5 cm

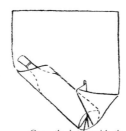

1. *Cover the bottle with the front side of the paper. Gather up pleats from one focal point on the bottom while folding the paper straight up.*

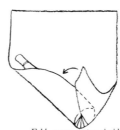

2. *Fold excess paper inside. Keep paper's lower edge in line with bottle. Roll bottle slighty to cover with paper.*

3. *Fold edge inside & secure with double stick tape. Creatively finish the bottle top wrapping.*

◆Wrapping a Bottle The Bottle version of Pleating a Cylinder.(Cf. Page 70)

●**Paper Size**

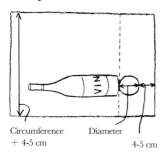

Circumference   Diameter
+ 4-5 cm   4-5 cm

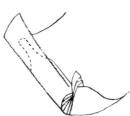

1. *Cover the bottle with the front side of the paper. Gather up pleats from one focal point on the bottom while folding the paper straight up.*

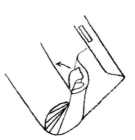

2. *Fold excess paper inside. Keeping the lower edge of the paper in line with the bottom edge of the bottle, roll the bottle slightly to cover with the paper.*

3. *Fold the edge inside and secure with double-stick tape. Use your creativity in finishing the top of the bottle wrapping.*

Pleating a Cup and Saucer

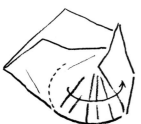

1. *Place the cup and saucer in the center and fold up the front side to cover, as shown. Pleat from the front to the right, gathering the paper at the center of the cup.*

2. *Pleat the other half in the same way, starting from the front. Gather the pleats at the top.*

Pleating a Bottle As for Pleating a Plate, but make "a" = height of bottle

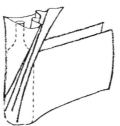

1. *Stand the bottle up on the paper. Pleat from the left to the center with both the front and the back paper.*

2. *Repeat on the right side. Finish by gathering the pleats as shown.*

Tying Techniques
— Classic Bow and Variations —

◆**Classic Bow** The very basic and most beautiful of all.(Cf.Page 12)

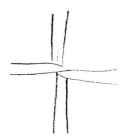 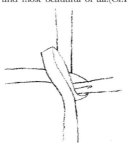 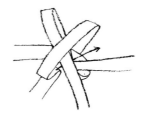 

1. *Pass one end under the other and pull snug.*

2. *Fold the lower end up along the upper and to form a loop.*

3. *Fold the upper end down and across the loop; fold and pass the fold beneath the first loop to form a second loop.*

4. *Adjust the loops to make a symmetrical, well-balanced bow. Cut off ends to suit the size of the loops.*

◆**Double Bow** This simple variation produces four loops.(Cf.Page 13)

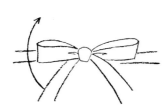   

1. *Create a Classic Bow. Lift the left end above the left loop.*

2. *Tie a second Classic Bow.*

3. *Hold all four loops close to their bases and tug tightly.*

4. *Arrange the loops attractively.*

◆**Pretty-side-up Bow** This technique is recommended for ribbons with distinct right and wrong sides.(Cf. Page 16)

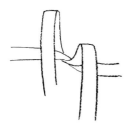 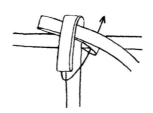 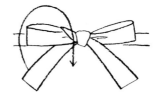 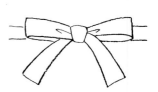

1. *Pass one end under the other and pull snug. Form loops with both ends so the right sides are out.*

2. *Lap the left loop over the right, as shown. Bring the left loop forward and under the right loop to tie the bow.*

3. *The underside of the ribbon will be showing on the left end. Twist to reverse it.*

4. *Arrange the loops attractively.*

The Classic Bow is basic. Simple, yet beautiful, it is appropriate for ribbon of any type. For best results, tie thin ribbons tightly, thick ones more gently.

◆**Classic Bow Variation** The center section becomes a longer cylinder in this variation.(Cf.Page50)

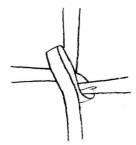 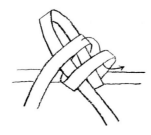 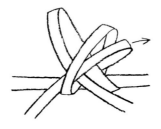 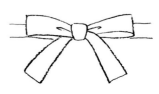

1. *Pass one end under the other & pull snug. Form loop with lower end. Pass upper end down, across, then beneath loop as shown.*

2. *Bring the upper end down and across the loop and wrap around twice.*

3. *There are now two loops circling the first one. Lift up the right-hand loop and pass it over the left.*

4. *Tug on the new right-hand loop to tighten the knot. Adjust to make a symmetrical, well-balanced bow.*

◆**Winged Bow** The simplest bow of all.(Cf.Page 24)

◆**Single-loop Bow** The one-loop variation on the Classic Bow. (Cf.Page 13)

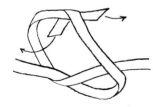  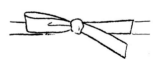 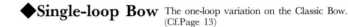

1. *Pass one end under the other and pull snug. Hold the upper end to face right. Pass the lower end above and below it, as shown.*

2. *Pull the left and right ends snug to tighten the knot, then pull them above it and trim.*

1. *Pass one end under the other and pull snug. Form a loop with the lower end. Pass the upper ribbon down and across the loop, then beneath it as shown.*

2. *Arrange the loop and ends. Trim the ends so that they are in balance with the size of the loop.*

◆**Sheaf Bow** Form a sheaf of loops, then knot.(Cf.Page 25)

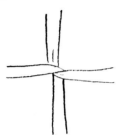 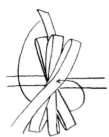 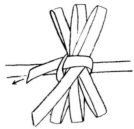 

1. *Pass one end under the other and pull snug, with the lower end much longer.*

2. *With the bottom end, form several overlapping loops, top and bottom, crossing at the center.*

3. *Bring the top end to the front, wrap across all the loops at the knot and around in back. Knot the ends together.*

4. *Adjust the sizes of the loops and plump them out attractively.*

Tying Techniques
Ribbon and Wire Techniques

◆**Crossed Loop Bow** This technique makes the most of lustrous iridescent ribbon.(Cf.Page 14)

1. Fold back the ribbon to the rear as shown, then bring to the front and overlap, to form a loop.

2. Make another loop below. Wrap a wire around the center, making gathers in the ribbon.

3. Wrap the wire around two or three times and cut off its ends. (Single crossed loop bow)

4. Repeat steps 1-2 to create a double crossed loop bow.

◆**Wired Loop Bow** These loops resemble a Classic Bow (Cf. Page 52)

1. With the trailing end of the ribbon, form a loop and cross at the rear.

2. Fold the trailing end to the front to form another loop, overlapping at the front. Pass a wire over the loops.

3. Wrap the wire around two or three times and cut off its ends. (Single set of wired loops)

4. Repeat steps 1-2 to create a double set of wired loops.

◆**Tying on a looped bow** The key point is to place the wired loop over the knot.(Cf.Page 15)

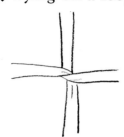 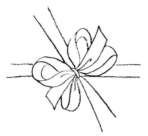 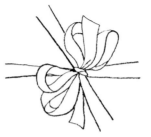 

1. With the same ribbon as you used to make the loops, pass one end under the other and pull snug.

2. Place the loops so the wire is over the knot.

3. Tightly knot above the wire. (With a Twisted Loop Bow, pass the ribbon through the central loop to knot.)

4. Bring the ties down beneath the looped bow.

These bows all use ribbon loops held in place with wire. Try changing the ribbon type or color—the possibilities are endless. Attach to the gift with a separate ribbon, or tape on directly.

◆**Figure Eight Bow** The classic way to keep ribbon's right side showing.(Cf.Page 42)

1. *With the right side of the ribbon up, form a rounded loop, overlapping in front.*

2. *Repeat below to form a figure eight. Secure at the center with wire.*

3. *Wrap the wire around 2-3 times, then cut off.(Single figure eight bow)*

4. *Repeat steps 1 and 2 to form a double figure eight before wrapping with wire.*

◆**Twisted Loop Bow** Twisting the ribbon enhances the effect.(Cf. Page 51)

1. *Form small loop at one end. Coil clockwise. Hold in L-hand. With trailing end in R-hand, twist as before, holding at center.*

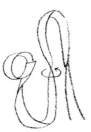

2. *Form two or three loops at the top and bottom, twisting each at the center point as shown.*

3. *Overlap large last loop (2× planned length of trailers) behind others, then secure (insert wire where thumb holds loops & twist).*

4. *Cut off the excess wire. Cut the last loop you made in half to form the trailing ends.*

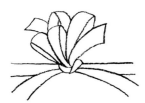

5. *Lift up the loops and tie tightly at their base.*

6. *Cut the ties to be as long as the loops. Or tie a Classic Bow with long ends.*

7. *Arrange so that the loops are well balanced. Overlapping them looks even more festive.*

Tying Techniques

These techniques add an extra touch of gaiety. Try them to expand your repertoire of bows and frills.

— Further Treatments for Bows —

◆**Perky Petit Bow** This technique puffs up a flat bow. (Cf.Page 60)

 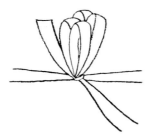 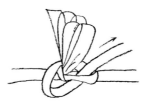 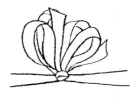

1. *Make a Classic Bow or Double Bow), leaving one rather long end.*

2. *Lift up the bow, circle its base with the long end, and pass the end through the loop thus formed.*

3. *Pull tightly on that end to draw in the base of the bow and make the bow stand up.*

4. *Adjust the ends to suit the size of the loops.*

◆**Ribbon Frill** This extra frill perks up a bow (Cf. Page 42)

 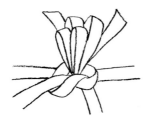  

1. *Complete a Double Bow.*

2. *Lift up its loops and ends. Drape a separate ribbon around its base and knot, as shown.*

3. *Tie a second Double Bow or a Classic Bow, keeping the loops the same size.*

4. *Arrange the loops attractively.*

◆**Inserted Bow** Two Classic Bows of separate pieces of ribbon, for double impact.

◆**Combined bow** Bring two bows together for a lavish look.

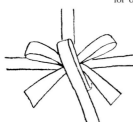  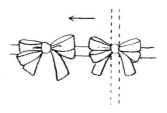 

1. *Complete a Classic Bow. Insert another ribbon through its knot and tie a second Classic Bow on the same spot.*

2. *Adjust the loops so that the second set is slightly smaller than the first.*

1. *Tie a ribbon around the package and tie a Double Bow. With a separate length of ribbon, tie a second Double Bow around the first ribbon.*

2. *Slide the second Double Bow up to the first so that their center knots are touching.*

Extra Accents

◆**Curling** This bouncy technique is an old favorite.

1. *Curl the ribbon over the edge of a scissors blade or a ruler.*

2. *For the prettiest curls, repeat several times.*

◆**Wave Loop Bow** A quick technique that's always handy. (Cf. Page 24)

1. *Form a thumb-sized loop and two more loops on both sides. Staple.*

2. *Fix in place with double-stick tape.*

◆**Wired Rose** The ribbon rose uses internal wires to hold its shape. (Cf. Page 61)

1. *Pull on the wire in the right-hand end to gather the ribbon.*

2. *Wrap towards the inside to resemble a rose. Wrap at the base with wire.*

◆**Wired Bow** Use hollow-woven ribbons.(Cf. Page 60)

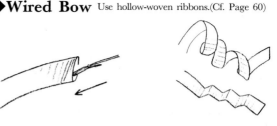 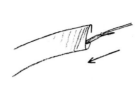

1. *Bend down the tip of a wire and insert in the hollow ribbon.*

2. *Curl, fold, or shape the ribbon.*

Tying Packages with Ribbon

◆**Crossed Tying** The basic technique, with the ribbon crossing at the center of the package.

 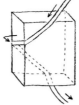

◆**Diagonal Tying** This technique shows off your lovely wrapping paper.

◆**Triangular Tying** This distinctive technique has great design possibilities.

◆**Single Tying** The simplest method of all.

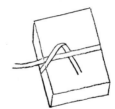 

● *Pages 22-23*

Ribbon・Classic Bow (Page 12)···❶、❷、❸

・Winged Bow (Page 24)···❹、❺

・Single-loop Bow (Page 13)···❻、❼、❽、❾
Reversible "peach skin" ribbon　No. 4586　38㎜、25㎜、15㎜　Col. 1

Wrapping Paper・"Bagging" It (Page 26)　WP001 Col. 16···❸ ❺
　　　　　　　　　　　　　　　　　　　WP001 Col. 49···❶、❻、❾

● *Pages 34-35*

❶　Ribbon・Classic Bow (Page 12)
Satin cord　No. 0927　Col. 15

❷　Ribbon・Double Bow (Page 13)＋Ribbon Frill(Page 42)
Satin-edged organdy ribbon　No. 4546　15㎜、25㎜、38㎜　Col. 00

❸　Ribbon・Classic Bow (Page 12)
Taffeta ribbon with satin edges　No. 4495　15㎜　Col. 2

❹　Ribbon・Single-loop Bow (Page 13)
Metallic ribbon　No. 4594　Col. 43

❺　Ribbon・Figure Eight Bow (Page 42)
Polka-dotted organdy ribbon　No. 4976　38㎜　Col. 2

❻　Ribbon・Classic Bow (Page 12)
Lace ribbon　No. 3119　Col. 12
Wrapping paper・Pleating a Plate(Page 40)
WP003　Col. 2

❼　Ribbon・Double Bow (Page 13)
Organdy ribbon　No. 1500　75㎜　Col. 12
Wrapping paper・Pleating a Plate(Page 40)
WP003　Col. 2

❽　Ribbon・Crossed Loop Bow (Pages 14-15)
Organdy ribbon　No. 1500　38㎜　Col. 2
Wrapping paper・Pleating a Cup and Saucer(Page 41)
WP008　Col. 12

● *Pages 54-55*

❶　Stuffed Toys　Ribbon・Classic Bow (Page 12)
　　　　　　　　Check ribbon　No. 4455　100㎜

❷　X'mas Tree　Ribbon・Wired Loop Bow (Page 52)
　　　　　　　　Check ribbon　No. 4461　100㎜

❸　Red Box Ⓐ　Ribbon・Classic Bow (Page 12)
　　　　　　　　Check ribbon　No. 4455　75㎜
　　　　　　　　Wrapping・Classic Box Wrapping
　　　　　　　　with Pleats (Page 77)

❹　Alphabet　　Ribbon・Wired Loop Bow (Page 52)
　　printed Box　Single-face satin ribbon　No.1150　25㎜　Col.72
　　　　　　　　Wrapping・Classic　Box　Wrapping
　　　　　　　　(Page 76)

❺　Green Box　　Ribbon・Classic Bow (Page 12)
　　　　　　　　Check ribbon　No. 4463　75㎜
　　　　　　　　Wrapping・Classic　Box　Wrapping
　　　　　　　　(Page 76)

❻　Red Box Ⓑ　Ribbon・Classic Bow (Page 12)
　　　　　　　　Check ribbon No. 4426　Col. 2
　　　　　　　　Wrapping・Classic　Box　Wrapping
　　　　　　　　(Page 76)

❼　Wheel　　　Ribbon・Classic Bow (Page 12)
　　　　　　　　Check ribbon　No. 4463　100㎜

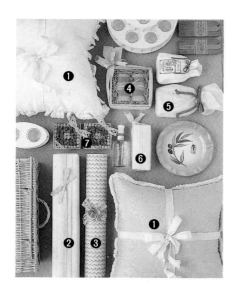

●*Pages 64-65*

❶ Ribbon・Double Bow (Page 13)　Wired taffeta ribbon　No. 10100　25㎜　Col. 510

❷ Ribbon・Classic Bow (Page 12)　Linen tape　No. 0369
Wrapping paper・Classic Box Wrapping with Pleats(Page 77)　WP015　Col.12

❸ Ribbon・Classic Bow (Page 12)　Linen lace ribbon　No. 0392
　　　・Wired Rose(Page 61)　Wire edged ribbon　No. 10200　25㎜　Col. 3,4
　　　　　　　　　　　　　Wired taffeta ribbon　No. 10100　15㎜　Col. 66

❹ Ribbon・Double Bow (Page 13)　Linen tape　No. 0371　15㎜
Wrapping paper・WP015　Col. 12

❺ Ribbon・Classic Bow (Page 12)　Linen tape　No. 0908　Col. 9
Wrapping paper・Pleating a Bottle (Page 79)　WP015　Col. 12

❻ Ribbon・Winged Bow (Page 24)　Linen tape　No. 0370　30㎜
Wrapping paper・Classic Box Wrapping with Pleats(Page 77)　WP015　Col.12

❼ Ribbon・Winged Bow (Page 24)　Linen lace ribbon　No. 0392

●*Pages 68-69*

❶ Ribbon・Classic Bow (Page 12)
Iridescent rayon ribbon　No. 4599　23㎜　Col. 16
Wrapping paper・Wrapping a Bottle(Page 70)
WP003　Col. 2

❷ Ribbon・Crossed Loop Bow (Pages 14-15)
Iridescent metallic organdy ribbon　No. 4617　25㎜　Col. 2,5
Wrapping paper・Petal Wrapping(Page 71)
WP006　Col. 33

❸ Ribbon・Crossed Loop Bow (Pages 14-15)
Iridescent organdy ribbon　No. 4563　38㎜　Col. 7
Iridescent metallic organdy ribbon　No. 4617　25㎜　Col. 5
Wrapping paper・Pleating a Bottle(Page 79)
WP006　Col. 44

❹ Ribbon・Classic Bow (Page 12)
Iridescent metallic organdy ribbon　No. 4617　25㎜　Col. 5
Wrapping paper・Classic Box Wrapping (Page 76)
WP003　Col. 2

❺ Ribbon・Winged Bow (Page 24)
Iridescent rayon ribbon　No. 4599　23㎜　Col. 16

❻ Ribbon・Classic Bow (Page 12)
Iridescent metallic organdy ribbon　No. 4617　25㎜　Col. 5

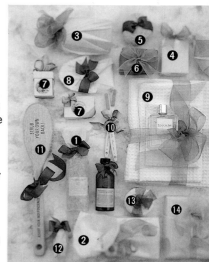

❼ Ribbon・Classic Bow (Page 12)
Wire edged ribbon　No. 10200　15㎜　Col. 11

❽ Ribbon・Single-loop Bow (Page 13)
Iridescent rayon ribbon　No. 4599　23㎜　Col. 16
Wrapping paper・Pleating a Plate (Page 40)
WP003　Col. 2

❾ Ribbon・Double Bow (Page 13)
Iridescent organdy ribbon　No.4563　38㎜　Col. 7

❿ Ribbon・Classic Bow (Page 12)
Wire edged ribbon　No. 10200　15㎜　Col. 11

⓫ Ribbon・Classic Bow (Page 12)
Iridescent rayon ribbon　No. 4599　23㎜　Col. 16

⓬ Ribbon・Classic Bow (Page 12)
Iridescent rayon ribbon　No. 4599　23㎜　Col. 2
Wrapping paper・"Bagging" It (Page 26)
WP003　Col. 2

⓭ Ribbon・Classic Bow (Page 12)
Iridescent organdy ribbon　No. 4563　25㎜　Col. 9

⓮ Ribbon・Wired Loop Bow (Page 52)
Organdy ribbon　No. 1500　25㎜　Col. 44
Iridescent metallic organdy ribbon　No. 4617　15㎜　Col. 2
Wrapping paper・Classic Box Wrapping with Pleats (Page 77)
WP006　Col. 44

Ribbons for special occasions

KUMIKO NAGAI

Publisher／TADANOBU SETO
Managing Editor／NOBUAKI SETO
Editor in Chief／KEIKO SEKINE
First published in Japan in 1993
Reprinted 1994
by NIHON VOGUE CO., LTD.
Copyright ©1994 NIHON VOGUE CO., LTD.
3-23 ICHIGAYA-HONMURACHO SHINJUKU-KU
TOKYO JAPAN 162-91